Flutter By, Butterfly!

Written by
Jill Atkins

When you go in a garden, park or field, do you ever see any butterflies?

Butterflies are insects that have six legs, four wings, 2 eyes, a head and a body.

Can you see the long, thin antenna on each side of this butterfly's head?

Butterflies eat mainly nectar from plants and flowers. But watch out for this white one – its caterpillar could eat all your crops!

When butterflies rest, they close their wings up, like this.

Butterflies go through four different stages in their lives, beginning with an egg. It's known as their life cycle.

Let's look at the life cycle of a butterfly.

The first stage

Eggs are laid in clusters on a leaf, like this.

One butterfly egg on a leaf

The second stage

Slowly, these eggs hatch into caterpillars.

Each caterpillar spends its days eating as much as it can, until it becomes fatter and rather sleepy.

The third stage

Then it develops into a **chrysalis**, like this.

While it's inside the chrysalis, a lot of changes take place.

The fourth stage

Then the chrysalis splits open and a butterfly emerges, like this.

Then it starts all over, with the female butterfly laying eggs once again.

There are many different kinds of butterfly. Here are a few:

The peacock butterfly – can you see the eyes on the wings? Do you think they look like the tail feathers of a peacock?

The blue morpho butterfly.

The red admiral butterfly.

The monarch butterfly.

This swallowtail butterfly is one of the biggest butterflies in the world.

Moths are similar to butterflies in many ways.

The life cycle of a moth is the same as for butterflies, except that the names of the stages are different. For moths, it's **egg**, **larva**, **cocoon**, **moth**.

Most moths fly at night, unlike most butterflies, which fly in the daytime.

Most moths fold their wings on their back when they rest, like this.

Moths are attracted to light and often fly up to bright things like light bulbs.

Some people don't like moths because they tend to flutter out of control when they are near a light.

Some people just don't like their hairy bodies!

Some moths could do harm in your home, by making holes in your jumpers and carpets.

The silkworm is the caterpillar of the Bombyx mori moth. Silkworms are important because they make silk. All the silk in the world comes from silkworms.

Silkworms feed on mulberry plants. Silkworms come from North China, but they are no longer found in the wild.

Here are some different kinds of moths:

Elephant hawk moth. You can recognise its caterpillar by the eye markings.

Cinnabar moth.

Winter moth.

Which do you like best, butterflies or moths? Can you explain why?

Which do you think is the best picture in this book?